Engage. Coach. Develop.

Building Strong Relationships That Drive
Individual and Team Performance

Artell Smith

(iUniverse®

ENGAGE. COACH. DEVELOP.
BUILDING STRONG RELATIONSHIPS THAT DRIVE
INDIVIDUAL AND TEAM PERFORMANCE

iUniverse books may be ordered through booksellers or by contacting:

iUniverse
1663 Liberty Drive
Bloomington, IN 47403
www.iuniverse.com
844-349-9409

ISBN: 978-1-6632-5117-6 (sc)
ISBN: 978-1-6632-5119-0 (hc)
ISBN: 978-1-6632-5118-3 (e)

Library of Congress Control Number: 2023912909

Print information available on the last page.

iUniverse rev. date: 12/20/2023

With Thanks

To Steve, Betsy, Lisa, Matt, Darren,
Brendan, Emily, Kaitlin, and Bryce

Legal Disclaimer

I'm not a lawyer, and nothing in this work should be construed as legal advice. Each situation is unique, varying according to the people involved and the context of the interaction(s). If you need legal advice, you should contact your in-house counsel or external counsel, as appropriate. The stories and examples presented in this work arise from my personal experiences. However, the names of individuals, locations, and companies, along with some details of the story, have been adjusted to ensure anonymity of those described herein. All hypothetical examples, as noted in the body of the text, make use of names, facts, and circumstances to illustrate the point. Resemblance to any real person or authentic fact pattern is purely coincidental. Where relevant, I have been granted permission to recount a story or some of its elements.

CONTENTS

FOREWORD

Lately I have been giving some thought to the notion of power in the workplace. It's an interesting fact of life in our organizations. CEOs, simply by being CEOs, have all sorts of power they're free to wield. This power is granted to them when they take the job. How they wield their power can make a tremendous difference in the culture of their organization, which is important because apparently culture eats strategy for lunch. (Or is it breakfast? I always forget!)

There is the old saying that power corrupts, and absolute power corrupts absolutely. It's an exaggeration, but there is certainly a hint of truth in it. Positional power can be abused, can be neglected, and can be handled incompetently. And the abuse of positional power comes with an amazing accountability escape hatch: the ability for those with power to blame others for their mistakes.

I think this is one reason why the title *manager* has negative connotations for some of us. When someone becomes a manager, she is given a certain amount of positional power along with that title. The manager influences our pay, our development, our career progression, who are teammates are, and whether we will survive a reduction in force. Some managers handle this power very well, others not so much. And those who don't often display their managerial incompetence by penalizing those who are doing the work. No wonder when I ask participants in executive education programs if they have ever had a bad manager, nearly everyone raises their hand.

The best managers I know do not care about their positional power. They know they have it, but they don't rely on it to do their jobs. They know it is a relic of an old command-and-control workplace paradigm. And they know it is fleeting, meaning it can be taken away as easily as it was given.

The best managers I know rely instead on what I would call *personal power.* Personal power is power granted to a manager based on her competency, integrity, attention, availability, and display of constructive behaviors. Personal power is granted a manager by others she works with, not conferred on a manager by some higher authority. And while positional power can be taken away, personal power is more lasting, more enduring.

I'm not suggesting that positional power is unimportant. I'm simply suggesting that it is overrated and is a source of much tension between managers and those who work with them.

Earlier I mentioned that I ask participants in executive education programs if they have ever had a poor manager and most answer that they have. I also ask if they have ever had a good manager, and similarly, most have. When I ask them to tell me more about what made those good managers good, only rarely does someone highlight some positional power trait. And that rare moment often has to do with the manager's relationship with more-senior people, being networked up the organization's chain of command for the benefit of the team.

But most of the time it is the characteristics associated with personal power that people use to describe their best managers. Those good managers are competent, caring, and resourceful. They're clear about performance goals; they partner with employees in their professional development; and they give straightforward and honest feedback. I could go on, but I'm sure you can add plenty of other, similar qualities yourself.

When Artell asked me to read early drafts of **Engage. Coach. Develop** and eventually asked me to write this foreword, I had already been thinking about the distinction between positional power and personal power. As I turned page after page in those early drafts, I saw Artell providing clear and succinct advice on how to accumulate and leverage personal power by engaging, coaching, and developing. And not just engaging, coaching, and developing those who are our formal reports, but engaging, coaching, and developing everyone we deal with in our organizations.

There is a lot of advice out there on how to be a good manager. Most of it is good, but a lot of it is overcomplicated and unnecessarily complex. For my money, simple, well-stated advice is worth its weight in gold. And within the pages of *Engage. Coach. Develop.*, there is plenty of gold to mine.

You know what makes a good manager? Knowing how to engage people. Knowing how to coach people. Knowing how to develop people. It's really that simple. Now, *how* to engage, coach, and develop: that requires some insight, tools, techniques, and trial-and-error practice. It's hard work, but the work can also be very gratifying.

That's why you are going to read *Engage. Coach. Develop.*, to build up your personal power and be one of those managers whom people talk about as being really good managers.

Enjoy the read. I certainly did.

Steve King

Steve King is the author of the following books:

- *Brag, Wonder, Worry, Bet: A Manager's Guide to Giving Feedback* (2013)
- *Six Conversations: A Simple Guide for Managerial Success* (2015)
- *Alignment, Process, Relationships: A Simple Guide to Team Management* (2019)
- *Prevention and Contingencies: A Simple Guide to Process Management* (2020)
- *The Manager's Dilemma: A Manager's Guide to Change Management* (2022)

INTRODUCTION

Models, Models Everywhere

I love human interaction models. It's fascinating to see how many ways people can come up with to accomplish basically the same thing. It's hard to choose which way is the best, however. Honestly, I'd have to think carefully about perhaps ten models and try to prioritize the top three.

But I'm getting ahead of myself. Business is full of models for everything from product cycles to pricing to consumer behavior. But what is a human interaction model? A human interaction model provides a structure to manage and analyze how human beings communicate with one another. While some models may use new and unfamiliar terms or descriptions, studying how people interact with each other to improve relationships at every level is not.

There is no one single model that everyone uses, but for organizational managers and leaders, models can help them tune into themselves more deeply and comprehensively to become more successful at connecting with the people they're helping develop. The way you approach your interactions will certainly dictate the strength of your relationships.

In my view, a solid human interaction model consists of the following:

- Guidelines that define a process describing how one human could or should interact with another using various techniques and tools.

- Identification of a context in which the interaction model is designed to operate, whether in normal daily life or in a business setting, or both.
- Description of desirable behaviors and outcomes likely to be achieved if the interaction model is used as designed.

That's a simple explanation, but anything more complicated would start to compare the models one against another.

First, let's consider some of the most groundbreaking interaction models in the last hundred years. There are a few candidates we should consider, to whet our appetite.

Perhaps *The Power of Positive Thinking* (1936) by Norman Vincent Peale? Or maybe *How to Win Friends and Influence People* (1952) by Dale Carnegie? I recently met someone who had become certified in the Carnegie Method. I won't lie, I was surprised. He was one of the few people I had ever met who had done that, and he was in his thirties.[1]

Strictly speaking, Peale's and Carnegie's works aren't really about the manager-employee relationship. They're more about the person-person relationship, regardless of position or status or context. Of course, these texts provide useful models for all the realms of human interaction because every relationship is person to person. But in *Engage. Coach. Develop.*, we're looking specifically at models for businesses and similar organizations, including nonprofit, educational, and government.

Perhaps Peter Drucker is the luminary we should credit? In 1973, Drucker published *Management: Tasks, Responsibilities, and Practices*, in which he says many profound things, among which is the thought that *efficiency* is about doing things right, and *effectiveness* is about doing the right things. Other authors and commentators have postulated, therefore, that efficiency is about management traits and that leadership is about effectiveness

---

[1] James B. Allen published his seminal work, *As a Man Thinketh* in 1903. See Sources at the back of the book for a full reference. I did not include Allen's book here for you to consider minutely because I felt some of his descriptions were problematic from an inclusion point of view.

traits. I don't know. I doubt Drucker meant that efficiency and effectiveness should be divided along manager and leader lines. But, setting aside that debate, Drucker did put forth a *manager* interaction model.

For organizational development professionals like me, Steven Covey's *The 7 Habits of Highly Effective People* is probably ground zero. I met Dr. Covey a couple of times. The first time was when I was a graduate student in the Marriott School of Management in the mid-1980s. I was walking through the business school building on a Saturday. One of the professors in the MPA program was with me, and we spotted Covey at the other end of the dark hallway wearing an understated and slightly crumpled tracksuit.

The professor I was with called out to Dr. Covey, and we walked down to him. Covey was a very congenial man. We chatted a bit about graduate school topics. At one point he turned to me and asked what I was going to do after graduation, and I mumbled through my answer.

This was before 1989, when *The 7 Habits* was first published, so Covey had not reached yet the level of fame he would eventually achieve. I knew him primarily from his first book, titled *The Spiritual Roots of Human Relations*. In my opinion, that book might be his best work. I'd encourage you to read it if you really want to know what motivated Covey and his thinking about interpersonal relationships.

To find what is most effective in the working world, we have to look a little deeper at what people want. Almost all working people are hoping for the "prize" to be conferred on them. The prize in my opinion is centered on an organization where people can use the skills they've acquired, do work they enjoy, in an organization that cares about them, with managers who appreciate their work and build them up for the future. Most everyone also wants to be rewarded appropriately, but we know that component is incredibly transient.

Is such possible? Can the prize be within our grasp? I believe so, yes. What does it really take to be successful, both for an organization and an individual? I think it's about selecting honorable relationship-building techniques and processes and sticking with them over time. If you will, an interaction model.

Many years ago, I knew a marvelous professor of physics at Cornell University. He held a prestigious chair and had been honored many times for his research. Sadly, he passed away too young. Somewhere in this brilliant man's past he had selected a human interaction model to use and stick to. It was very effective, and I saw him use it repeatedly and consistently. This is my summary of his model:

1. Exhibit thoughtful curiosity
2. Offer opinions/advice, only if asked
3. Regulate emotions intentionally
4. Be vulnerable

It was a winning combination of interaction techniques for him. Maybe for any of us! I think persistence and consistency are key.

Could any model work in an organization? Well, maybe not **any** model. In a 2010 **Harvard Business Review** article titled "First, Let's Fire All the Managers," Gary Hamel makes the argument, paraphrased by me, and possibly overstated, that managers are such an incredible drag on most organizations that doing away with them is the only rational choice. Hamel writes that guiding people to the higher road of self-management is the correct way to approach the problem arising from humans interacting with each other in an organization.

Hamel is probably right. There's a huge benefit to empowering employees, especially the kind of empowerment where the seeds of genius-level innovation and accomplishment could possibly be planted. Hamel goes on to lay out the characteristics of a self-managing organization and makes very persuasive arguments. All I can say is, wouldn't it be nice?! I don't doubt his research. But in my experience, it is very unlikely that managers could be eliminated. Yet the practice of management, and individual manager behaviors, can always be improved.

Over the years, I have tried a lot of different manager interaction models on for size and have found that most of them have some benefits. My purpose in writing *Engage. Coach. Develop* is to give you my thoughts on how to tune yourself up and connect deeply and effectively with the people on your team and in your organization. I will not try to debunk or cast aspersions on other interaction models. They all have their merits.

Managers, leaders, and others should regularly feel the need to throw a fresh coat of paint on their personae in order to keep things pertinent and interesting. This is not about changing your personality or other hard-coded behavioral characteristics. Finding the right type of paint and reinventing yourself is more about the reality of the changing workplace. Have you noticed that new employees are getting younger and younger? Me too. Some are so young that I must look twice.

Work hard to understand the mindset, skills, and personalities of your employees. If you do so, you will benefit greatly. So will your team and the organization. I've come to realize that continuous reinvention is an absolute necessity for me. Out with the old me and in with the new me, reinventing my manager interaction skills every (darn) day. Or so it seems.

I tell a lot of stories in *Engage. Coach. Develop.* They're all true, but I have fiddled with the facts, timelines, locations, and organizations, and of course I have changed personal names to protect individual privacy. I hope you enjoy this small contribution to the study of human interaction models.

*

Artell Smith is also the author of *No Time to Waste—Microbehaviors: Leveraging the Little Things to Become a Better Leader* (2023).

1

A Primer—Engage. Coach. Develop.

Being a Manager Isn't a Walk in the Park

A few years ago, I spent time with a group of managers who had all assumed new management roles recently. Some had been managers before, but for most it was their first time. They were all from the same organization, and my job was to help them improve their people management skills and behaviors. We talked about the basics: building relationships, driving performance, and meeting objectives. I offered them some thoughts on how to fulfill these critical manager responsibilities.

I was feeling *OK* about the training, but I wasn't feeling *fulfilled*. That was troubling. I like to leave a group of managers better off than I had found them, but this wasn't shaping up that way. The mood of the group had a tinge of despair to it too. I pressed them a bit, telling them what I was sensing, and I heard several things in response:

1. Discouragement over the number of business processes they were still individually responsible for, in addition to being accountable for people management. They had been

promoted from subject matter expert positions and had not been relieved of any technical/process duties.
2. Confusion about how to build comradery on their teams since employees ran the gamut of generations—Gen X to Gen Y, boomers to millennials. They were struggling to identify the best tactics to foster strong, productive connections. They deeply felt the problems and challenges of poor intercultural interactions as well.
3. Dismay because of inadequate support from their own managers. The managers of managers were working hard to transform many different aspects of their business model, not just doing people management. As a result, the managers felt neglected, and their problems minimized.
4. Fatigue due to organizational change. They were all struggling to muster enthusiasm for building up the teams for which they'd been given stewardship in the face of so much current and heralded change. Most felt they were in a no-win situation and had reduced their overall efforts accordingly.

These four items are weighty. Managers who don't have enough time to manage, who struggle with generational and cultural differences, who feel unsupported by their own managers, who are fatigued by change, and who are disengaged generally, are going to struggle, and they were. More than one learning and coaching session was necessary to uncover all the issues and brainstorm solutions! There are ways to address all these common challenges, plus others.

Where is the best place to start? Daniel Pink, in his book *Drive: The Surprising Truth about What Motivates Us* (2009), suggests that focusing on autonomy, mastery, and purpose (AMP) will greatly advance the cause of engaging and retaining employees. Giving employees the freedom to control some part of their work, the resources to deepen and expand their expertise, and the possibility of attaching themselves to a higher purpose—well, that's a beautiful thing to behold! Engagement and retention should be a by-product of this approach. Please read Pink's book for terrific ideas and counsel.

Engagement

Because *engage, engaging, and engagement* are generally overused in the work setting, we need a way to distinguish between these devilishly similar ideas. For the purposes of *Engage. Coach. Develop.*, engagement is a state of being that includes engaging conversation, coaching, and development. It's not the result of a single incident but of applying the principles mentioned herein.

I'm using the word *engage* differently and in contrast to *engagement*. For example, a statement such as "The employees in our retail business all have high engagement!" is generally interpreted as a good thing and represents an amalgamation of experiences and environmental factors that led up to this pronouncement.

Here's what I mean:

- I'll use *engage* as a noun in the sense of "Starting the meeting out with an engage will set the right tone. Let's talk about our favorite team outings." The usage of *engage* as a noun might be new to you, but you'll get the hang of it.
- I'll use the verb *to engage* to indicate positive action by managers to honor and retain their employees. I engage. You engage. She engages. We engage. They engage.
- I'll use *engaged* or *engaging* as an adjective that modifies a noun, in the sense of "This engaging meeting will go a long way to improving [employee] morale." There is a hint of process in this too.

The other two words of this three-faceted approach, *coach* and *develop*, don't present the same challenges as the word *engage* does. Coaching is coaching, and developing is developing. Certainly, there are different kinds of tactics used for coaching and developing that we'll explore, but those tactics are all recognizable as being attached to the words.

Simple Definitions for Engage. Coach. Develop (ECD)

The ECD approach uses three elements—engaging employees, coaching them, and developing them in a way that encourages them to become the best they can be. That might ring trite in your ears, but I don't intend for it to. Over 165 million people participate in the civilian workforce in the US, most of whom I'm sure want to do the best job they can! And most all workers have a manager hopefully helping them to do so.

At the center of the ECD approach are your employees. It's all about them. True, there is mutual benefit to be derived, but I would consider that to be a positive by-product, not a starting position. If your employee receives and responds well to coaching and development, it will spur you, the manager, to even greater levels of investment in terms of both time and money. You can engage an employee, coach an employee, and offer an employee development, but if the employee takes a pass on those things, then you won't have much to work with.

Let's look at each component of ECD:

Engage

You engage employees as you have direct and frequent interaction with them. All employees desire and deserve a cordial and productive relationship with their manager. Managers should want the same. It's not rocket science, but it does require steady effort. The little things count in this endeavor, for example, upbeat conversations and one-on-one meetings that are not focused on tasks alone. The big things count even more, like solid support from the manager when trouble arrives, plus a commitment to have employees' backs. Engaging employees, as a general concept, looks different when viewed through the lens of the many available interaction models.

Coach

You coach employees over the long run when you provide confirming or developmental feedback. Coaching is not an event; it is a process in which you and your employees are both invested. Employees want to hear from their managers about what they're doing well and what they need to pay more attention to. Employees usually enjoy transparent and open dialogue with their managers. Managers should try to accentuate the positive when coaching employees. Jack Zenger and Joe Folkman, in their book *The New Extraordinary Leader: Turning Good Managers into Great Leaders* (2019), pitch their tent on the idea that employees go farther and faster when their existing strengths are accentuated through coaching, versus only focusing on their weaknesses and areas in need of development, which doesn't lead to the same outcome. I intend the same thing as Zenger and Folkman when I use *coach* throughout this book. By the way, I hope you'll read Zenger and Folkman's book, now in its third edition.

Develop

You develop employees when you provide opportunities for them to gain or improve skills, to excel, and to win. Engaging and coaching both require your time and attention but make no mistake: developing requires investment. Stated simply, employees need a plan—a plan to move forward, acquiring new skills and abilities along the way. I've seen some development happen randomly or unexpectedly. This isn't usual and can't be counted on. Rather, intentionality is required. One way to think about intentionality is to consider that developing employees takes much more time than it does to simply coach them. I'm able to provide coaching and feedback that will either reinforce or correct behavior more or less immediately. But if you wish to see employees thrive by learning a new skill, then focused, tangible investment is required, such as providing a detailed development plan, pairing them with subject matter experts for a significant period of time, or sending the employees to formal training.

Employees Deserve Your Best Efforts

Using an ECD-oriented approach will improve your relationship with employees. They need your best efforts and are, in fact, counting on them. More than once when in meetings with other senior leaders, I've said the following: "Employees who don't know us, and whom we may never meet, are hoping that leadership is having frequent conversations about how to make their lives better." I didn't make the observation to chide the leaders present, but rather to bring to the forefront of their minds that one of the basic purposes of leadership is to make things better for employees. Whether such a task turns out to be hard or easy, this truth should carry leaders forward. Managers don't always have as much control over the larger organizational environment as leaders do, but they certainly have a significant amount of influence over day-to-day team environment.

It seems to me that it's easy for an organization to drift—and for employees to drift along with it. Once, in a moment of true clarity, I realized that the company's drifting and my drifting were two different things. I may not have much control over what the company is going to do, but I certainly have control over my own behaviors. And as a manager, you too have a lot of influence on the team and its members.

Here's a real-life ECD example:

Just prior to a major downsizing, resulting from an acquisition, I was in a meeting with my fellow managers lamenting the loss of so many talented employees. Most of us in the room had been asked to stay with the new organization, but we had also been given the task of assessing a portion of the employee population to determine who would be invited to stay and who would be asked to leave.

About half of the employees who had been entrusted to us were to be downsized. As people managers in both the current and future organization we made a collective decision to create a positive difference in the lives of employees throughout the downsizing process. By staying focused on the needs of employees, we were able to accomplish the following:

1. We **engaged** with those who were leaving to keep them continuously apprised of what was happening, the timeline, and to address their concerns as best we could. We engaged with those who were invited to stay to encourage them to do so, answer their questions, and visibly show we cared about them.
2. We **coached** employees who were leaving to help them transition their duties to others, and to prepare for job searches, if applicable. We coached those who were remaining to help them transition to new duties and new managers, and to deal with survivor's guilt.
3. We **developed** departing employees by offering them job search training, resume preparation, and education on how to claim government benefits. We developed those who were continuing with the company to ensure that their long-term orientation would be matched with the right learning and mentoring investments.

Many positive things resulted from this attention to detail. And to be clear, we used our approved interaction models to execute against ECD components. Employees who left expressed their gratitude for the caring way in which the situation was handled. Employees who stayed did the same thing, with the added commentary that watching how we interacted with departing employees was critical to their decision to remain with the company.

Cautionary Tale—Feeling Left on an Island

Not all outcomes in times of organizational disruption are so positive. You can probably think of times when you were subjected to a situation at work where some ECD-aligned interactions could have gone a long way to improve your overall satisfaction. I can think of a couple of occasions when this was true for me.

I once had a manager who decided to abruptly leave the company we both worked for. The manager was a long-service employee and well-respected, so his decision to leave caught me off-guard. For the couple of years I reported to him, we'd been fully occupied in advancing the cause of new business offerings. It was exciting work, and I really enjoyed my growing relationship with the manager.

I've reflected many times on this situation over the years. My consistent conclusion is that that my manager missed an opportunity to help me and his other direct reports who were "left behind."

How could the leader have honored the three-part mantra of engage, coach, and develop having made the personal decision to leave? What he could have, or might have, done is purely speculative on my part since only he knows the reasons for the fast departure. I know I have pondered the events over the years partly because I immediately missed him!

Using the ECD format, I came up with three sets of questions my manager could have used with me and others the answers to which may have eased the blow of his unexpected exit.

Engage

1. "What worries you most about my immediate departure?"
2. "What help can I provide to you in your transition to a new manager?
3. "What can I do for you personally?"

Coach

1. "Whom could I align you with in the company as a guide to help you through the complexity of this change?"
2. "What are the issues you'd like immediate coaching on and advice about?"
3. "How frequently would you like to meet before I depart and what topics would you like to cover?"

Develop

1. "What skill gaps could prevent you from being successful in your personal transition? Which gaps would you like my help with?"
2. "What formal or informal learning experiences do you want to make a priority right now?
3. "What career conversations would you like to have before I leave?

The above questions could be adapted to many internal transition situations where employees need their managers to be particularly attentive.

2

How to Engineer Engaging Experiences

It's easy for me to say that you should focus more time and attention on creating engaging experiences for your employees. I assure you I'm not being naïve. In day-to-day work life, this can be hard to do. However, engaging experiences are the start of everything good. Without them, you cannot build the trust and rapport necessary to coach and develop employees. Creating engaging experiences starts with you and your mindset.

Creating a Positive Mindset That Will Help You to Engage Employees

While the war to engage with your employees is won one battle at a time, there is a conflict playing out in your mind all the time, specifically, via your mindset. Psychologists know that mindset is slow to change, and then only after long and specific effort. I worked with a senior leader who once said in a meeting that the word *feel* should never be used at work. And he wasn't joking. Honestly, I don't think butter would've melted in his mouth. In keeping with my smart-alecky self, I responded, "I don't *feel* you're right about that." My smart mouth didn't do me any good. I got a withering look. But still, he was wrong in what he'd said. Feelings of all kinds are part of work life, including empathy, compassion, love, hate, indifference, and apathy—a full spectrum of emotions that can easily become evident.

In the crusade to create engaging moments with your employees, you might need to adjust and refine your mindset so that your actual behavior aligns with the positive impact you desire. Over my years in HR, I've heard from many employees who are struggling with their managers. The three items I hear the most: (1) my manager is overly critical, (2) my manager never recognizes me for my good work, and (3) my manager doesn't listen to me. That's a trifecta of mindset issues that could prevent managers from engaging their employees in positive, uplifting interactions, full of hope and promise.

Psychologists tell us that our brains are predisposed to negative thinking and pessimism. Why? Because the vigilance that comes from a negative bias helps the species survive. And survival is important no matter what age you are or what experiences you've had in the past. To put a fine point on it, predispositions lead to behavior. If the predisposition is bent toward negative thinking, then behaviors will be cut from the same bolt of cloth.

The process of mindset regeneration is greatly expedited when you cultivate self-compassion. I'm sure I won't do this concept justice on my own, so I'll borrow a few brilliant thoughts from Stanford researcher and psychologist Emma Seppälä. For us to make meaningful progress in adjusting our mindset, Dr. Seppälä recommends that we substitute belief in our strengths with a belief in our ability to put forth effort and that we substitute self-compassion for self-criticism.

I believe Dr. Seppälä is saying that having a strength(s) is not a "destination," which has the tendency to create limitations. For example, I was coaching a sales executive once who said to me, he was a "one trick pony." Meaning, he had one leverageable strength in the workplace, with a set of skills attached, and that's all he could do. I don't believe that's all he wanted to do, yet he had boxed himself in very tightly. My purpose in speaking with him was to explore a potential next step in the company. I didn't get very far. Had the sales executive adopted the mindset of "putting forth effort" to acquire a new strength perhaps he would not have shut me down so fast.

The other component of Dr. Seppälä's work suggests that we must abandon self-criticism and embrace self-compassion. Recall the negative bias our brains are automatically equipped with? This is that. A negative bias which exists out of concerns over potential failure and impending doom can lock us in place, like the sales executive above. The killer combination of a belief in our ability to put forth effort and regenerate ourselves, plus a bias to cut ourselves some slack on a more frequent basis, will help us to find more ways to positively connect with others.

Be kind to yourself and grasp the idea that you've made and will make mistakes, and so will those around you. Cultivating a mindset as described here, one of both hope and positivity, will serve you well as you reach out to your employees and engage them in an effectual dialogue that builds a long-lasting relationship.

I'm sure I've greatly oversimplified Dr. Seppälä's wisdom, so I suggest you research her work yourself for more information or pick up her book *The Happiness Track: How to Apply the Science of Happiness to Accelerate Your Success* (2017). Also, please check out the Sources section at the back of the book for more recommendations.

A Simple Process for Engaging with Anyone

Engagement is a state of mind, but it is not the same as "an engage." As you may recall from chapter 1, I stated that I would be using the word engage as a noun. A tangible interaction. Think of the engage as a gift that you give to a person or a team. The engage allows you to start an interaction on a positive footing. A good engage can also keep a relationship moving forward if you've hit a bumpy patch.

A solid engage between you and your employee helps create and sustain an environment that fosters comfort and trust. A series of positive engages over time create rapport. Once rapport is established, a sincere coaching relationship, plus targeted development, can begin. The state of mind of engagement is produced as an outcome of the engage process.

When it comes to engaging with a specific person, here are a few simple guidelines:

Always begin on the human side. Get to know the person in context. Be appropriately curious, and make sure that you listen carefully to what the employee says. Build the interactions one upon the other, and gradually deepen the conversations based on what you've already learned. Steady, applied effort will give you clues as to what "human side" means to the individual. For example, many people think that I do (or should) care about sporting events: football, baseball, and basketball. Turns out, I don't. Not even a little bit. The human side for me would include a discussion of science fiction movies and Asian food restaurants.

Create a pattern that becomes a routine. You and your employee should speak regularly about work life and nonwork life. Don't push the nonwork life conversation too hard, and don't pry. Allow yourself to be guided by the employee. Casual and informal is what you're shooting for in these interactions. Create a sense of comfort that contributes to increased trust. While some people like to keep a strict separation between their work and nonwork lives, I have encountered very, very few people who enforce this rule all the time.

Establish and confirm the interaction rules and follow them. As you establish a routine, you'll come to have a knowledge of the ground rules by which you must operate. Think of these as the rules of engagement, no pun intended. You should engineer your conversations so that you can easily switch between the topic of work, projects, progress, and the routine components of life outside of work. How about purposely engineering some interesting experiences with the person? A casual team event, or one-on-one lunch, will give rise to stories to reflect and build upon.

If you're starting from next to nothing in terms of relationship, think about these questions and statements to kick-start an engaging interaction:

1. You're new to the team, but we've both been with the company (or profession or industry) for a few years. I bet you've gone on fun outings with other teams. I'd love to hear about one. I have a few stories too. Let me start the ball rolling with a very memorable experience I had.
2. I heard from someone that you play the piano. Cool! I'm not a very good keyboardist, but I do love to play the guitar. What kind of music do you like to relax with?
3. We've been working on this presentation for hours. I'm tired. Let's grab a soda and talk about something else, anything else. Have you ever traveled outside the country? I know you speak Spanish, so I'm wondering if you've visited any Spanish-speaking countries.
4. You saw the new Marvel movie last weekend too? It wasn't what I expected, but I really liked it. What did you think?
5. I love Italian restaurants! The one on Main Street is a favorite. What about your favorite restaurants in town?

The foregoing statements and questions are easy and straightforward—as would be any variations on the themes—and should promote quick dialogue. How do you choose the content that will work best? I'm not sure I can help you there. I mean, it'll be very person-specific and based on whatever clues you've gathered.

If you really don't know the person at all, I suggest that you start asking questions about hobbies, music, sports, home state or country, prior experience, and so forth. That way, you get clues to consider immediately. No clues? Ask someone who does know the person, including a recruiter, a prior manager, or simply a friend. They'll help you out, and before you know it, you'll have engineered a worthy engage.

Example of a Regular Engage Process

I've worked with an excellent consulting group for the last few years. The first time we met together to get acquainted was a very positive experience for me. I was impressed with their skills and experiences. It was easy to form relationships with each of them individually. At the beginning of the meeting, the lead consultant asked us about any hobbies or outside interests we had. Refreshing. We put on the table a few to consider, e.g., going to the movies, reading books, diving, gaming, walking through cemeteries, and enjoying various types of cuisine.

At the beginning of every meeting since the first one, we started out with a similar discussion. It was a nice way to get things moving and ease into the business discussion with positive feelings. The consulting group members also do a good job of remembering who liked which kinds of activities. I'm the cemetery walker, for example. The consultant I interacted with the most always asked me about what cemeteries I'd been to recently, and I gave him a quick summary.

Overcoming Resistance

There is no requirement that employees must reveal anything about their nonwork lives to managers. Some employees have one reason, or potentially many reasons, not to discuss their personal lives at work. You should honor that, of course. On the other hand, I can think of two exceptions that are worth exploring:

Introverted Employees

No doubt you have worked with people who were introverted. While any number of personal preferences can be at play, the natural personality style of such a person can have a chilling effect when it comes to verbal interactions. In such a situation, I recommend that you start out with simple, but direct, communications about the work itself, mentioning how information will be shared in terms of progress toward meeting business objectives. A discussion about team interaction expectations may also prove to be valuable.

Email, or any other asynchronous technology, may be the best medium for communicating with a very introverted employee, at least for some period. In my experience, it is rare for jobs to be structured to enable the indefinite use of asynchronous communication. When in doubt, ask this question: "What are your preferences for communicating with me, and how do you want to update me on your progress toward completing your individual and team goals?" Then, listen carefully to what the employee says!

Suspicious or Angry Employees

You will at some point face a situation where, through no fault of your own, an employee on your team will be suspicious of your motives for using engage techniques. Beyond suspicion, which can be full of emotion, your employee may simply be angry about ... well, anything and everything. For example, your employee could be angry about perceived or real slights, or conflicts that occurred on previous teams or with previous managers. This can give rise to a particularly tricky dynamic.

My suggestion would be to employ these three tactics: (1) maintain transparency about what you, the manager, are endeavoring to transmit to the employee; (2) acknowledge that there are some things you don't know or fully understand but assure the employee that that you are here to help make the situation better; and (3) continue with an ongoing focus on the work itself. Past grievances can be eventually dealt with, but not always. You should always feel enabled to focus on the work the employee needs to get done, and how they will do it.

A Manager's Effort to Engage That Started Well and Ended Badly

My close associates and friends know that I'm a bit sarcastic, which sometimes gets me into trouble. The best way to handle me when I get in a smart-alecky mood is to give it back to me as good as I'm giving. Not everyone is comfortable doing this, so I need to be thoughtful. I recall one moment with a manager that didn't work out very well. Chloe was her name, and we worked together a total of two years at a large organization.

We'd been in a meeting, and I'd made a mistake while doing some calculations. Chloe jumped in and defended me in front of the more-senior business leaders, saying, "We've been throwing a lot of new things at Artell. I should've been providing more help and guidance." The comment made me instantly more comfortable with my relationship with Chloe. I felt that it was a breakthrough of sorts since she was an introvert and hard for me to read. The rapport that I felt we'd already had was strengthened because of her rising to my defense.

The next day, we were debriefing the meeting. I said something along the lines of, "I usually make ten mistakes a year, and that was only my first. Hopefully the next nine won't be so bad!"

Chloe, after giving me a measured look, said, "We don't like mistakes here. And we also don't like smart alecks." Except she didn't say *aleck*. And there was not one shred of humor in her voice. I got the message immediately, and it chilled our relationship. I was glad for the advice, but not the way it was delivered or how it made me feel. Not an effective engage. From then on, I was wary around her. This is something you want to avoid creating in your employees because it hinders engagement.

Common Wariness Creators and Possible Alternatives

If you want to avoid making an employee wary, which is the first step to degrading rapport and eroding trust, try the suggestions that follow (for which I've also provided a suitable alternative that should help stave off negative reactions):

1. Admonishing employees in front of their peers using abrupt and embarrassing language, like this: "Darren, the data you presented was from the wrong database. You should be more careful and ensure that we are dealing with the correct story when making decisions!"

   ✓ Instead, try this: "Darren, I'm wondering about the database you used for this presentation. I'm definitely not an expert. Could we go a little deeper into the source of the info before we decide?"

2. Injuring an employee with faint praise. This is a bit more subtle, but it causes you to end up in the same negative place. "Emily, you've been doing such a great job, and I appreciate your efforts. But I don't understand why this report is so far off the mark."

   ✓ Instead, try this: "Emily, your efforts on this project are much appreciated. How are you feeling about our process and results?"

Other wariness creators include things such as changing assignments or moving deadlines abruptly without offering an explanation, refusing a request to meet with higher-up management, and using harsh or coarse language in a way that suggests the employee did something wrong.

A Note about Motives and Employees' Interpretation of Your Actions

A close colleague of mine, who is a private person with a tendency toward introversion, once chided me after a class I facilitated about my unrelenting extroversion, especially when I'm in front of a group. I'd made a comment to the group, who were mostly managers, that getting to know someone personally is frequently the key to building a strong, lasting relationship. My colleague was worried that I was suggesting that managers could or should put undue pressure on their employees to open up. And, worse, that it was somehow an expectation of employees to discuss their non-work lives.

She made a very fair point, enlightening me to something that I needed to correct. When I say you should get to know you're employees personally, here's what I'm thinking:

- Gain a basic understanding of their nonwork circumstances
- Appreciate any stated cultural alignments and beliefs
- Develop a degree of insight into personality style and general mindset
- Gain clarity on definitive opinions or behaviors

When my colleague and I discussed the foregoing items, she reemphasized that a manager needs to be careful not to step across a line and ask questions that could feel invasive and intrusive or be seen as having an ulterior motive.

My extroversion has sometimes gotten the best of me. I usually run my life as though I live in a glass house. Everyone can see what's going on in my life, and I'm not shy about sharing details. But not everyone wants to metaphorically live in a glass house. Some questions, posed with a genuine desire to understand another person, may land in the wrong way and cause offense or worse. What's a safe way to begin?

In situations where the individual is completely unknown to me, other than a name, I always start within the context of our first encounter. For example, if the employee is new to the team, I talk about the team and its work. Then I inquire about past team experiences, asking what was good and what was bad, and try to discover the person's preferences. I have a logical business reason for doing this, namely that I want the team the person is joining to continue to be high functioning. Knowing team and individual interaction preferences is an enormous help. If in a conversation I sense reluctance to go further, I stop dead in my tracks. Pushing on and inquiring about life, family, hobbies, etc., would be dumb.

In subsequent conversations, I may tread into new areas, such as food, entertainment, sports, music, or books. These are generally safe topics that will provide insight. Once you find some common ground, you may be able to gradually expand the boundaries of the conversation to include other aspects of the person's life. But if you are not able to expand the range of these one-on-one discussions, then make do with what you know. Even one area of discussion can be fruitful for many conversations. Keep chipping away. But don't push or pry. The right to privacy is a real thing!

Consider a couple of examples, drawn from my past. The first part of each of these two scenarios describes the actual situation, and the second part of each scenario describes what should have happened:

- **Kate**

  The Negative, Actual Scenario

  Kate was unhappy with her current assignment. She had not been consulted before being moved to a new team and had been given assignments that exceeded her skill set. In the last coaching session, Kate's manager told her she was dangerously close to being placed on a performance improvement plan. Kate reacted with a considerable amount of negative emotion to the coaching and requested a sit-down with HR and her manager to lay out her concerns. One session was not enough to get to the bottom of the situation.

Several meetings later, Kate's story emerged. Literally, no member of management had ever tried to engage her and speak plainly to her as a valuable employee with growth potential. There was no meaningful plan, much to the chagrin of the manager. Kate's continued employment was in doubt, not because of poor performance, but because of a lack of any positive, engaging interest from her current and former managers. She eventually left the company for greener pastures.

The Positive, Alternate Scenario

Kate enjoyed her work with the company. She had a run of three managers, each of whom had shown an interest in her as a person. Kate's first manager was still in regular contact with her and checked up on her at least quarterly. They went out to lunch at a place that Kate had pointed out was a favorite of hers and spent a comfortable hour talking about whatever was on her mind, whether work or private life.

Kate's second manager was really focused on her development. When a new position came up that fit with Kate's career path, the second manager connected the dots and introduced her to the hiring manager. Kate was reluctant to leave the team since it had been very rewarding developmentally and socially. But the plan they'd agreed upon included this type of role. Ultimately, she interviewed for, and was offered, the job.

The second manager and the third manager coordinated an excellent transition for Kate, and she now felt at home on her new team.

- **Damien**

The Negative, Actual Scenario

Damien had been with the company for more than ten years working in a production area alongside many seasoned employees. These veteran employees, including team leaders and managers, barely knew Damien, partly because he was somewhat introverted, and partly because his English skills were rudimentary, in their view.

The lack of any engagement efforts during most of his years on the production floor created a long delay in his professional growth. Since Damien had few or no true friends at work, he didn't have anyone to confide in or to look out for him. When new positions and developmental opportunities came up, the lack of sponsorship prevented him from knowing about them. It was easy for him to ultimately leave the company, seeing so little progress.

The Positive, Alternate Scenario

Damien started to learn English in his native country, and by the time he reached the United States, he was conversational but hadn't learned any technical or mechanical vocabulary. Upon being hired, he spent thirty minutes with his new manager and a couple of the team leaders who'd been at the company for many years.

Since Damien was new to manufacturing, they checked in regularly on him. Developmental opportunities came around from time to time that Damien eagerly accepted. He was offered classes in English, which he took advantage of. The plant director heard about Damien and his good work, as well as his potential. When an appropriate supervisory position became available, Damien applied and was selected for it. Damien is now thriving at the organization with other possible, more advanced positions in his future.

I wish I could say that Kate and Damien are unusual cases. But they aren't. Interest in the employee as a person and intentionally working to build rapport goes a great way toward producing positive, satisfied emotions in the employee and ultimately a receptivity to being coached and developed. The recipe for Kate and Troy could be the same recipe you use with many of your employees.

When You Should Call HR

Any individual manager's motive to get to know team members should revolve around business performance and continuity. You don't need to be bashful about asking questions that help you to understand the factors that could negatively impact production, deliverable creation, operating standards, timelines, processes, technologies, etc. Running the business is always your job, and you are entitled to ask questions of employees to understand if the work of the organization is going to be negatively impacted. Simple rule is this: when in doubt, contact your HR department.

Here are a few types of situations that should always prompt you to call HR:

- Physical or mental health problems
- Personal legal situations, including divorce, child custody, etc
- Alleged discrimination, of any kind
- Grievances against other employees, managers, or leadership
- Alleged violations of policies, rules, regulations, or laws

Be as empathetic as you can when you first learn about an issue. You don't have to put yourself in the role of judge and jury, but you do need to know how to direct an employee to the right resource.

The rapport that comes from consistent engagement takes time and effort, but it's worth it. Think about the individuals with whom you interact daily. How many of them do you think you have true rapport with? What does rapport look like and sound like anyway? The word that comes to mind first is *comfortable*—the comfort that comes from knowing that you can discuss most, if not all, things and that you can trust the person to keep confidences. Easy, unforced communication is a hallmark of rapport.

Using any communication channel opens the possibility of producing the same positive feelings. Do you have texting buddies or Facebook buddies? Some know you better than others, I would wager. But a constant flow of easy communication sustains relationships over long periods of time, and that is the key to creating the environment for coaching and development.

3

How to Coach for Amazing Results

I've always enjoyed contemplating this Chinese proverb credited to Lao Tzu and found in his book the *Tao Te Ching*; "When the student is ready, the teacher will appear." Wouldn't it be nice if such were always the case! There are many elements of truth in this proverb when it comes to coaching in an organizational environment, namely, coaches and coaching make no sense without someone willing to be coached. The employee's manager is most often the coach.

A coach's purpose is to help an individual or team to do something differently or better. In school sports, young or inexperienced players are still learning the game. Perhaps a player has real potential but isn't aware of the current or future skills required to realize that potential. Enter the coach who points all this out and brings the best out of the athlete. We are all like that player in a sense, with all the potential to become our best. This can be true in any field of endeavor. It's easier to be our best when we have the support and help to get there. I believe the same idea of coaching applies to the workplace, the individuals in it, and the teams that are composed of those individuals *who have something they need to do differently or better.*

There's no best way to coach; there are a thousand best ways. Once the need for a coach is clear, the way to coach must be discerned, the best way being dependent on the needs of the individual or team. Some require light touches; some, heavier. Some require short periods of time to achieve objectives, and some are on lengthier timelines. Most of the people I have coached over the years have experienced a customized version of myself, suitable to the coachee. I never assume that the coaching will be the same, from one person to the next.

In the Introduction, I mentioned that there are many manager interaction models to choose from. Most of the interaction models include a coaching component, but I'm not going to propose a specific coaching model for you to use or create a new one to offer for your consideration. What I will do here is review what I can only describe as a values-based approach to coaching. Like engagement, the best coaching starts with you and your mindset, the objective being for you to be the best version of a coach you can be. I suggest you spend some time with these principles before you start providing either confirming or developmental coaching to either an individual or team.

Great Coaches Are All Around Us; You Can Be One Too

One of the classes I teach for new managers includes a module on coaching. Participants in the class are provided with opportunities to explore the best way to build relationships with their employees. Even though they're inexperienced, they usually know what it means to engage an employee, and they recognize the need to coach employees to greater levels of sustained performance.

If you're currently in a coaching relationship, as either a coach or a coachee, you know that coaching involves some sort of progress. That is, when the result of coaching is improved performance, success is measured against a set of objective criteria. There's certainly room for subjectivity in many coaching relationships, but both the coach and coachee know that some specific behaviors and results are the hoped-for outcome.

What does it really take to be a great coach? I've never been disappointed with the following activity to sketch the basics of excellent coaching behaviors. You could use this simple process with your team or an individual coachee.

Activity—What Makes a Good Coach?

Think about the people who have made the biggest difference in your life from a personal, work, or career perspective. The person could now be, or might have been in the past, a manager, peer, subordinate, friend, or family member. Of the people you are contemplating, who really got it right when it came to (1) coaching you through difficult challenges, (2) coaching you on what you needed to further develop, or (3) coaching you on specific behaviors or outcomes? (It's possible you may not have thought about the person as a coach at the time!)

Answer the following questions about the person who is top of mind:

- What is the single most distinguishing behavioral characteristic that made the person so effective at coaching you?
- From the perspective of demonstrating empathy, what could you count on the coach to always do (or not do) when you were together?
- How did the coach make you feel before, during, and after your interactions?
- What did the coach inspire you to do better or differently?
- What successes did you achieve?
- In what ways have you tried to emulate the coach in your current day-to-day interactions with colleagues, friends, family members, or others?

In a learning environment, after participants answer the above questions, I ask them to work together in pairs and compare notes. There are usually many commonalities in the answers given. Of course, this is the point of the exercise—to demonstrate that great coaches share many similar characteristics, regardless of the specific skills or behaviors being coached.

You may not be surprised to know that many participants offer up a coach from their younger years, frequently the coach of a team sport like basketball, football, or baseball. Some offer up a music coach of some kind, including voice or instrument. And, of course, some offer up a coach from a current or past work experience. The positive statements offered most frequently about these great coaches are as follows:

1. "The coach cared about me as a person."
2. "The coach inquired about and was interested in all parts of my life."
3. "The coach humanely pointed out the things I needed to improve upon."
4. "The coach reinforced the things I was doing right."
5. "The coach recognized my achievements as I improved over time."
6. "The coach was nonjudgmental despite the fact that I made mistakes."
7. "The coach continued to care about me after the coaching ended."

This is quite a list of positive behaviors, right? It would certainly be amazing, too, if all of us could become such great coaches. But there's something more: When many of the participants described the experiences they had with their coaches, emotion was evident in their voices. They smiled too, with softened gazes as the memories came flooding back. It's really a great experience for me as the instructor to listen to these stories.

Anyone who takes the time to coach another person ultimately desires that person's success. Using my long experience in organizations (yes, I'm old), I've come up with three coaching principles that I've settled upon. You may wish to consider these principles in the context of your current and future coaching relationships.

Principle I: Learn to Enjoy People for Who They Are Right Now

Truly caring about someone requires jettisoning the propensity that we humans have to judge others with often very little to go on. Sure, it's easy to discover a trait or characteristic in someone else that discourages you from getting to know them better. This is when you need to try harder. Pick out something about the person that you find intriguing. As you feel your curiosity and interest grow, you'll be able to frame questions whose answers will likely propel you to greater empathy and caring. Do this, and the rest of the path will be much easier to walk.

A few years ago, when I worked at a large multinational, I needed to build a collaborative relationship with someone who was my indirect report and who, I believed, was standing in the way of an important global project. This person, Butler, was adamant that the work I was doing was unnecessary and likely to cause harm to employees in the country where he lived.

Butler and I had a few interactions that can only be described as collisions. I wasn't happy, he wasn't happy, and I was having a difficult time trying to find something about Butler that I liked. I could see some of what he was worried about, but I was inflexible in terms of seeing the picture his way. I felt that he and I were going to have many unhappy conversations as we butted heads on a regular basis. I did not believe my coaching abilities were equal to the task.

One day when I was feeling the project was going nowhere and that my influence skills were insufficient, I sat down and started to write a list of a few things that I really enjoyed about Butler. Why? Who knows! Let's just say inspiration came to me that I should.

What I enjoyed about Butler included his strong sense of purpose, his understanding of the commercial business, his relationships of mutual trust with business leaders, and his operations/process mindset that was among the best I'd ever encountered. Yikes! There were plenty of reasons to enjoy an association with Butler, but all I could do at that point was endure the conflicts he and I were embroiled in. That needed to change.

The next conference call I had with Butler, I asked him more transparently, more caringly, what he hoped would be the outcome of the operational model he was currently managing on behalf of several thousand employees. He explained to me his vision, and I saw that it was *somewhat* aligned with my vision. Yet there was still a great distance between our two perspectives.

Instead of continuing to push my point of view, I started to ask many more questions about both his vision and his day-to-day work life in the western European country where he lived. The more curious I got, and the better the questions I asked, I was able to begin to appreciate the various points he made. I didn't agree with everything he said, but there was certainly more agreement than disagreement.

At the next earliest opportunity, I flew to his country, and we spent a few days together working and socializing. Butler's family was very interesting, and we chatted freely about many things. Then Butler told me about the career aspirations of one of his children, which was coincidentally the same career aspiration as one of my children. My relationship with Butler improved greatly. He and I began to enjoy one another for who we were, fellow travelers on the planet.

Eventually, Butler accepted a position to join the global team, and together we created a very effective operational model that served employees in seven different countries and was durable enough to last multiple years. You could describe me as Butler's coach, but he coached me too since I had a lot to learn about the European business. Our coaching discussions were very free-flowing and amiable. We innovated together, and I grew to respect him very much.

If I had stupidly pursued walking down my original path of reckless conversational collisions, I'm not sure what would have happened. Among other things, I'm pretty sure I would have lost out on having a friend. I also know that separately, Butler and I would have achieved much less than we were able to achieve together.

Questions to Help You Get to Know and Enjoy Your Coachee

To learn to enjoy people for who they are, you will need to acquire more data. That sounds impersonal, but I don't mean it to be. If you have more than a few people on your team, you'll need to get good—and fast—at data acquisition. There are many questions you could ask to discover helpful information. Please don't use all these statements or questions at one time. This isn't an exercise in speed dating!

You should be detecting an overlap with the first part of ECD, namely, "engage." The following questions can also be used as part of an engage with an employee. But all engage experiences do not result in coaching moments. Since we are talking specifically about the coaching part of ECD, you should think about these questions as introductions to the coaching experience.

- "Tell me about the best job you've ever had before coming here."
- "Tell me about the best day at work you've ever had."
- "Tell me what puts a smile on your face at work."
- "Tell me about a project you were sad to see come to a conclusion."
- "Tell me about the best class you ever attended at work."
- "Tell me about the best team you were ever on, and why it was special."

The information you gather, using these or other questions, will prove invaluable as you get to know the person on a deeper level. Note that none of these questions has a task or process orientation. That data comes about through the normal operational processes of the team. Also note, I stayed away from nonwork questions and suggest you do the same in the early stages of a coaching relationship.

The setting is important too. If you have an office, have these conversations on the *same side* of the desk. Don't create artificial separation with a desk in between the two of you. If you're in a cubicle environment, find a conference room, or better yet share a meal and a drink. If you're in a virtual environment, use a fun background or make sure you each have a drink and a snack to enjoy. Whichever way you go, and whichever questions you ask, keep the atmosphere light and airy.

Principle II: Make Emotional Intelligence Your Superpower

If I were to lead a brainstorming session with the question "What is the most important set of behaviors for a manager to have?" I would certainly hope someone suggests the behaviors associated with *emotional intelligence*.

Dr. Dan Goleman went a long way toward explaining emotional intelligence in his path-clearing book *Emotional Intelligence: Why It Can Matter More than IQ*, which was originally published in 1995.[2] Goleman wasn't the first to investigate emotional intelligence, but he certainly succeeded in popularizing the concept. His book paved the way for a resurgence in leader and manager development efforts, and its main idea has become a core concept in almost all management models I know of. Goleman's five elements of emotional intelligence are self-regulation, self-awareness, motivation, empathy, and social skills.

There are other emotional intelligence models, as mentioned. I recommend that you look at *The Handbook of Emotional Intelligence: Theory, Development, Assessment—An Application*

---

[2] The most up-to-date version of Daniel Goleman's *Emotional Intelligence* is the twenty-fifth-anniversary edition, published in 2020.

at Home, School, and in the Workplace (2000) edited by Reuven Bar-On and James D. A. Parker.

There are a dozen or more research-oriented publications and websites where you can read even more on the topic of emotional intelligence. Most of the emotional intelligence models you come across are legitimate points of reference and will help guide you through conversations wherein you're working to demonstrate the best behaviors possible.

Based on my experience teaching leaders and managers about emotional intelligence, I'm going to summarize what I think are some of its core mandates:

1. Understand your impact on others.
2. Keep control of yourself in all situations.
3. Hesitate before speaking.
4. Prioritize the needs of others over your own needs.
5. Support and sustain the motivation of others.
6. Be positive and genuine.
7. Be authentically curious.

I hasten to add that my emphatic statements, above, are not based on my own academic research. Rather, they're based on my experience in many organizations over four decades in the business world.

It takes a lifetime of dedicated work to master these seven elements of your emotional quotient. After all, like Rome, **you** were not built in a day. But all the behaviors suggested by these elements should be part of your long-term strategy to become a better manager, leader, and person.

I've personally always struggle with 3. above. "Hesitate before speaking." If you know anything about the Myers–Briggs, then you'll understand what I mean when I say that I'm a recovering ENTJ. This personality style has no trouble jumping into a conversation without much forethought. A hallmark of people with the Commander personality is that they tend to leap before they look and speak before they think. It takes very little to get ENTJs going, but sometimes quite a bit to get them to stop. I've been working on this behavior for a long time, it seems, and have made modest progress. Every interaction is an opportunity to practice!

Principle III: Value the Person and the Relationship More than the Desired Skills

The core of coaching is to always value the person, the relationship, ahead of the skills you're hoping the individual will develop. It's a little trickier to extend this logic to valuing the person ahead of the organization. Generally, I would say you should value the person and the relationship more highly, though there are exceptions.

I'm a *Star Trek* fan, maybe even a *Star Trek* nerd. I don't have a tattoo of NCC-1701 anywhere on my body, but I'll admit that I've thought about getting one.

One famous scene in *Star Trek II: The Wrath of Khan* contains some often-quoted dialogue between Mr. Spock and Captain Kirk. Spock has just entered a highly radioactive chamber in which he performs a vital task to save the *Enterprise*. Spock quickly succumbs to the radiation. The exchange goes as follows:

> SPOCK   Were I to invoke logic, logic clearly dictates that the needs of the many outweigh the needs of the few.
>
> KIRK   Or the one.

This famous interaction gets flipped around in *Star Trek III: The Search for Spock*. In this situation, Captain Kirk has been searching for the regrown and reanimated Spock on the Genesis planet. At last, the two friends are reunited, and this dialogue ensues:

> SPOCK   My father says that you have been my friend. You came back for me.
>
> KIRK   You would have done the same for me.

SPOCK   Why would you do this?

KIRK   Because the needs of the one outweighs the needs of the many.

I bet you see where I'm headed now!

The first item on the list I suggested as a summation of the "what makes a good coach" activity was this one: "The coach cared about me as a person." What does that really mean in practical terms? Digging deep into everything we know about the psychology of relationships, we find interesting, relevant tidbits. Healthy and caring relationships are based on trust. This is a two-way street, of course. The coachee needs to trust the coach, and the coach needs to trust the coachee. Yet the coach is in the power position, without a doubt.

Your coachee will trust you and believe you care if you exhibit interest in the person apart from the stated objective, which is likely about developing important skills, modeling specific behaviors, or achieving certain objectives. This should all be obvious because in our personal, nonwork lives, there are people we trust implicitly and about whom we care deeply. Research suggests that there is a tight relationship between trust and caring, with sets of behaviors for each becoming self-reinforcing for both.

In the book *The Culture Question: How to Create a Workplace Where People Like to Work* (2019), we learn that leaders who have established trust with an employee are the very same leaders who demonstrate they care about the employee. The authors conclude that the best way to develop trust is to care about employees. Since I'm not an expert on the connection between trust and caring, I recommend you pick up a copy of *The Culture Question* by Eric Stutzman, Randy Grieser, Michael Luban, and Wendy Loewen— or download the digital or audio version—and learn more about how these kinds of behaviors can also positively influence your organization's culture.

Here are some specific ideas of my own creation for how to demonstrate that you care about an employee:

1. Accept the employee for who they are, without judgment, regardless of gender identity, race, ethnicity, national origin, culture, language, religion, creed, etc.
2. Ask the employee respectful and thoughtful questions, and then listen intently to the answers.
3. Express concern about any difficult situations confronting the employee and offer support and assistance as circumstances allow.
4. Show appreciation for the employee's contributions in such a way that they will recognize your sincerity.

No set of strategies is foolproof, of course. If you're in the middle of a turnaround situation with the employee, you must ease into all the foregoing four strategies. Jumping in with both feet could backfire on you. Approach things gradually.

Coaching the Hero, Not Being the Hero

It's sometimes challenging to redirect one's coaching efforts in terms of exhibiting the right skills at the right time for the right reasons. Many managers are selected for their positions thanks to their expertise and success: they're often considered the heroes who have solved a difficult problem. Being an expert doesn't really mean you can be a great coach. Here's the key issue: your days of being the hero might be over. Let's explore this hero concept a bit more.

One of my best friends and most cherished colleagues is Betsy Hagan. I met her more than twenty-five years ago when we worked together at a human resources consultancy and outsourcing company. Thanks to our mutual friend and mentor Steve King, who wrote the foreword for *Engage. Coach. Develop.*, Betsy and I are again working together at the Center for Professional and Executive Development, Wisconsin School of Business, at the University of

Wisconsin–Madison. In our roles there, we each teach sections of one of the marquee programs offered called Manager Boot Camp.

A couple of years ago, Betsy started describing an aspect of developing others that centered on how leaders and managers should be the coach of the hero, not the heroes themselves. Betsy wrote a short monograph titled "Becoming the Hero's Coach,"[3] which I'm going to present here with her support and permission.

[3] Betsy Hagan, "Becoming the Hero's Coach," Wisconsin School of Business, Center for Professional and Executive Development, September 8, 2018, https://blog.uwcped.org/becoming-the-heros-coach/.

Becoming the Hero's Coach by Betsy Hagan

It's a rite of passage in most organizations that if you're at the top of your game as an individual contributor, you're likely to be tapped to take on people management at some point in your career. This happens for several reasons, sometimes because it's the only promotional path to increase pay for high potentials, sometimes because of a shallow pool of managerial talent within the organization, and sometimes because high-performing individuals crave the authority and power that is perceived by being *the boss*.

Unfortunately, the well-honed skills that define a great individual contributor don't always translate to the skills needed to lead people. Studies and surveys done over several years have suggested that organizations often base hiring and promotion decisions on an employee's experience and performance in her current role, and then reward the employee by giving her an entirely different role! Per the research, an alarming 80 percent of the time, this methodology backfires.

Organizations large and small should create learning experiences for managers that will help build the skills those in transition need to acquire to avoid being part of that 80 percent failure club. But even when good people skills are developed, success can be elusive unless newly minted managers shift their mindset from being the *hero* as an individual contributor to the *hero's coach* in managing others.

New managers must go from being the person who does stuff to being the person who facilitates and supports a team of people doing stuff. They must go from thinking about getting things done themselves, to thinking about developing other people's skills and talents so that those people can get things done. They must go from solving problems to helping their teams solve problems and supporting them in growing and becoming better at what they do. Here are some tips for shifting the old-school manager mindset:

From Player to Coach

It's so tempting to *just to do it yourself*. Resist that loud voice in your head that says it takes too long to explain and teach others. The value you bring as a manager is to enhance the skills and capabilities of those around you. You can't do that if you aren't willing to coach others.

From Doing to Serving

As a manager, you focus on the needs of each team member. Your job is to help them succeed and do their best work. This means you recognize the individual strengths of others and actively find ways to help them demonstrate those strengths.

From Me to We

As individual contributors, we likely have built up our sense of identity around our well-honed technical skills. We may have grown accustomed to receiving recognition for our contributions. Great managers know that they often must step back and let others share in the limelight of recognition.

Leadership is about inspiring and enabling others to do their absolute best together to realize a meaningful and rewarding shared purpose. The best leaders find success and satisfaction when they shift their mental mindset and motivation from being the hero to being the hero's coach.

Thanks, Betsy! This is excellent advice for both managers and experienced individual contributors. Knowing that you are not the most important person in the coaching relationship is the beginning of wisdom. Whether we think of our careers as long or short, we should all be working to develop the next generation.

There's no question that coaching people can be rewarding for everyone involved. When you create and maintain a state of engagement, honor who people truly are, use emotional intelligence, and value people, you'll be able to help people develop.

4

How to Develop Your Employees

Hiding directly behind the word *develop* is the word *grow*. If proper development is offered employees they will take full advantage of it, in my experience, and they will grow. Skills improve, tasks become easier, judgment becomes more solid, and future opportunities become available. The notion of developing is something that not everyone likes the sound of. It requires nontrivial work effort! The rewards can be great, however.

In Steve King's book *Six Conversations*, he lays out the following half dozen critical questions that all employees deserve an answer to from their manager:

1. "What is expected of me?"
2. "What and how should I develop?"
3. "How am I doing?"
4. "How did I do?"
5. "How will I be rewarded (and recognized)?"
6. "What's next for me?"

I hope you'll pick up a copy of Steve's book and read about all six questions, but for right now, let's focus on the second question— "What and how should I develop?"

Essentially, via this question, employees are inquiring about the skills required to meet the expectations of the manager, the team, or the organization. A manager does not need to wait for employees to ask the question. In fact, on-the-ball managers will frequently discuss with employees the essential skills, knowledge, and abilities needed to be successful on a regular basis.

The topic the manager needs to ponder is whether the employee possesses the necessary skills to be successful, and if so, are they strong (enough) and "fit for purpose"? *Fit for purpose* means that the employee can do the specific work that is assigned. Answering Steve's "what and how" question points the conversation toward growth and ensures the employee will have the support required to achieve important personal development goals, plus the goals of the team overall.

In some cases, the answer provided to the development question will also help in determining a career path or at least career trajectory. If the question is asked and answered, then the next step would be to prioritize the order of skills acquisition.

All of Us Can Learn New Skills

Learning agility is highest when we are very young but tends to decrease as we get older. There are two reasons for this: (1) the individual's mindset calcifies and begins to resist learning new things, and (2) partly based on mindset, the neuroplasticity of the brain decreases, and it physically becomes harder to learn new things. I suspect this is why I am having such a hard time learning Spanish in my 60s, while the French I learned when I lived in France in my 20s is as accessible as ever.

We're talking here about neuroplasticity, which is not a word that slips easily off the tongue. It's very useful for you as a professional to know about neuroplasticity and the benefits of maintaining or increasing it as you work on developing new skills, whatever age you might be. It's also important for you to know because of your role as manager/coach. You'll be able to offer encouragement to employees who may resist development or believe they simply can't do something new. (Recall my story about the sales executive in the previous chapter.)

The official definition goes something like this: neuroplasticity is a comprehensive term applied to the brain's ability to restructure itself by forming new neural connections throughout life. High degrees of plasticity allow the brain to reorganize itself by forming new neural connections. The neural network that is your brain can change and grow based on new situations or changes in the environment.

While in some cases the neural reorganization is thrust upon us by way of injury or disease or circumstances, the reorganization can also be prompted intentionally by doing things such as reading fiction, learning new words, learning a new language, learning how to use your nondominant hand for tasks, traveling, creating art, and remaining curious. Cool, right?

Example of Neuroplasticity: My Sister Ruth

A couple of years ago, my older sister Ruth suffered a somewhat severe stroke. It did not leave her incapacitated physically. She was able to move freely enough, with a slight "hitch in her git-along," as my mom would say. But the stroke did wreak havoc with some of her long-standing skill sets, for example, her ability to play the piano.

Ruth had to relearn how to play the more complicated piano pieces she had known for many years. The work was tiring and frustrating, but she was making progress; new neural pathways were being created that essentially bypassed the damaged ones. Her physician had explained this to her early on. It was essential for her recovery.

Though we don't realize it, we are forming new connections in our brains all the time. You can even make this a habit. If you search online for neuroplasticity, you can follow the search returns to the origin of the concept in the 1890s. You'll discover some surprising tidbits, including the roles of Carl Jung, Adolf Meyer, William James, Emil Kraepelin, and Sigmund Freud in developing the concepts of neuroplasticity and realizing the developmental potential of the human brain.

Excellent research has been done on this topic. I recommend to you Christopher Lee Bedford's doctoral dissertation, titled *The Role of Learning Agility in Workplace Performance and Career Advancement* (2011), published by the University of Minnesota.[4] In basic terms, Bedford's research says that you really need to be able to learn new things in a disciplined and orderly way if you wish to get ahead. *And so do your employees.*

Based on my experiences, here are a few learning agility behaviors, promoting neuroplasticity, you could work into your routines:

- Show curiosity in new topics, skills, or endeavors, and develop the ability to formulate coherent, open-ended questions about them.
- Listen in a reflective and reciprocal way, thereby allowing yourself to ingest and organize new information.
- Exhibit a willingness to set aside, at least temporarily, any preconceived notions of how the world works based on prior experiences and established mindsets.
- Develop the ability to navigate ambiguous situations with objectivity, patience, and a high degree of emotional intelligence.
- Hone your ability to remain self-motivated in difficult or paradoxical situations, while applying creative and innovative techniques.
- Develop the ability to manage conflict and reduce tension in yourself and others, especially when the act of learning produces frustration and anxiety.

---

[4] Currently unavailable in book form, but downloadable from the website for University of Minnesota Libraries Digital Conservancy, https://conservancy.umn.edu/.

I imagine that none of this information comes as a surprise to you. It should give you comfort to know that succeeding at helping someone to develop is contingent upon that person's learning agility. The foregoing set of expected behaviors gives you something to keep in mind when speaking with employees.

Discovering the Right and Most Important Skills for the Employee

Aligning strategy, people, and skills is not a new idea. Ed Gubman, PhD, wrote eloquently about this in his book *The Talent Solution: Aligning Strategy and People to Achieve Extraordinary Results* (1998),[5] which he published when I was a new employee at a human resources consulting and outsourcing company. One of my critical tasks as a new manager of learning and development was to create a competency model that was attached to the company's strategy. Ed's work proved to be a godsend since he had done much research and thinking on the subject.

This kind of integrated and comprehensive alignment, from business strategy to employee skill set, is very popular in the current management literature. For example, a few years ago, the head of human resources at a large technology-centered company sent a letter out to thousands of its employees around the world stating that the employees' current skill sets would likely no longer be needed by the company in five years. Such a pronouncement could not have been made if there hadn't been a deliberate alignment of market, business strategy, talent, and specific employee skills.

If you were one of the employees receiving such a letter, you may have been tempted to descend into despair or become angry. *Who's to say my skills won't be valuable in five years? I've been*

---

[5] *The Talent Solution* is no longer in print, but you can obtain a used copy or a Kindle version via various online suppliers. Even though many of the examples in Gubman's book are dated, the book provides great value by helping the reader to understand the thought process behind the aligning of strategy and people.

here for two decades, and the company has always needed me and what I am able to do!

Um, well, that's the point, isn't it?

Employees can fool themselves into thinking they'll always be valuable. But no one skill is durable forever, and most skills are being changed out for others quickly nowadays. What I really like about the letter that was sent to employees, though, is that it offered each employee the opportunity to retrain during the five-year interval and gain skills that the company predicted it would need. Genius! A terrific development and retention strategy.

Creating a Personal Development Plan

We're ready to look at the personal development plan (PDP) an employee needs to be individually successful and help the team and organization prosper.

PDPs should be written down and include a timeline. Writing the plan down allows both you and the employee to see what has been attempted and accomplished when you evaluate the results. The employee and the manager should develop this plan together. While the manager can and should think about what might be best for the employee, the manager should not by any means approach the creation of this plan as an opportunity to tell the employee what it is she *must* do. That would mute any rapport that had previously been created and erode trust.

But you already know that. After having cultivated a state of engagement, you are familiar with who the employee truly is and what she would like to do. Here's a simple example to consider:

A company I'm familiar with decided it needed to venture into a new business, similar to, but not the same as, what it had been doing for multiple decades. Business leaders arrived at this decision based on an analysis of market trends and what clients wanted to buy. After the analysis was complete, the company decided on its new product set and on the talent needed to execute on the strategy. Many skills were then identified as being requisite for employees to learn. The highest-priority skills in this case were digital acumen and project management.

The business need was clear, and now the talent in the organization had to be curated and then aligned to that need. As mentioned, the paramount skills in deficit were digital acumen and project management. The action of creating a development plan may seem daunting, but really all you need is a new email screen, a new Word document, or a clean piece of paper. Create these sections:

1. business need
2. required skills
3. assessed skills gap
4. methods for filling the gap
5. milestones
6. timeline
7. progress check-ins

Next, you need to know who the experts are in the organization who can play the role of coach, instructor, tutor, or mentor. Last, you need to know who will play the role of accountability partner. This could be you, the manager, or someone else. Either way, the essential elements of a PDP are now in place.

To continue with the example of the company entering a new business, in writing PDPs for employees, they placed strong emphasis on taking classes, either in person or online, completing cognitive-behavioral evaluations, watching videos, engaging in behavioral role-playing, and participating in expert employee coaching. Linkages were made throughout between the required competencies and the behaviors. Descriptions of good/better/best behaviors became an area of focus for on-going discussions. Third-party assessments were also employed to give some comfort to both the manager and the employee that the right skills were actually being developed.

This was a somewhat lengthy endeavor, with the initial phases approaching nearly two years. Why so long? Because the entire process needed to be followed, from determining the market, to developing the individual skill set, to achieving skill proficiency. You may not have such a long journey in front of you when it comes to identifying the skills. If you're employed by a business or organization whose mission is clear, whose products and services are obvious, and for which talent has been identified, then really all you need to do is set down the plan with your employee. Consider this conversation between a manager and an employee about development and growth:

> MANAGER   Thanks for meeting with me today, Clara. We're going to continue our conversation about your development plan.
>
> CLARA   Sounds good to me. I'm still confused about where I'm going to find the time. My schedule is packed. What could I stop doing so I can focus on learning new skills?
>
> MANAGER   I agree we need to sort that out. And I promise we will. Let's talk about the new skills first, OK?
>
> CLARA   Sure. The fact that the business is beginning to move in a new direction is exciting. But I don't see my connection to it. What I do here on this team is far removed from the new direction.
>
> MANAGER   I partly agree with that, and it's why we need to think about your skill set and get a development plan together. As you know, we're transforming the company to be a player in both the technology services and consulting business. You're an excellent developer, and I see that you could become a consultant.

CLARA   Got it. But I'm not all that fond of talking at length to people, which seems like it would be a big part of a change in positions. I'm worried it might be too big of a stretch for me.

MANAGER   But you already do some consulting with internal groups, and that is something we can build upon. Plus, your project management skills can be worked into program management skills.

CLARA   I'm open to trying. I trust your judgment in this. Where do I start?

MANAGER   Let's start with the formal education. I would like to enroll you in a few consulting skills and program management classes, pending your agreement. Each is three days in length. There are openings next month and the month after.

CLARA   That's super. So, the company is willing to spend money on developing my new skills?

MANAGER   Yes. But there's more to the development than just classes. The rule of thumb is that you should spend 70 percent of your time doing the new work while learning along the way, 20 percent of your time being actively coached by an expert, and 10 percent of your time in formal education.

CLARA   I know there are experts in the consulting area. Are you thinking that I should start to spend some time with them? How about Christopher? He's a really good guy. Smart.

MANAGER   Funny you should mention him. Christopher is one of the people I have in mind. Again, if you agree, I'd like to have you spend one day per week with Christopher, following him around and working on some of his projects.

CLARA   I need to be honest. This is a much better conversation than I imagined. I was expecting you to say that I'd need to learn about all of this on my own time.

MANAGER   No, no. Maybe this was the policy once upon a time at the company, but no longer. We need to retain our best talent and not let our clients down with high turnover and under-developed skills.

CLARA   OK. Fair enough. I've liked working for you, and I have no reason to doubt. We've covered the 10 percent and the 20 percent; now what about the 70 percent?

MANAGER   This is trickier. It would require you to move out of your current role and into something that approximates what we have in mind. We need to put a development plan in place for Sanchez. He's your backup, but he's not quite ready for your job.

CLARA   We should talk to him together. He trusts me but doesn't really know you.

MANAGER   Perfect. Let's get you moving along the road we've agreed upon. I'll take first pass at the plan, and then you can look it over and revise as needed. Sound good?

CLARA   Let's do it.

Working together with employees to create a PDP facilitates buy-in. Don't hold out on what you think might be essential. Be comprehensive without scaring the employee into inaction.

Prioritization with the addition of a timeline will go very far toward creating focus coupled with just the right amount of urgency.

And don't be afraid to change the plan if the one you have agreed upon isn't working. The goal is growth, and you'll know from engaging with employees over time whether they are growing and happy.

5

Bringing It All Together

In a Circle, in a Hoop that Never Ends

Thanks to Disney's *Pocahontas*, I have a way to describe how engage, coach, and develop all interact. "In a circle, in a hoop that never ends." Because the English language pulls us from left to right, we tend to think of the item at the far left of a phrase or process as the beginning. "Start here," so to speak. In the case of engage, coach, develop, this is not true, except maybe once: the very first time you meet someone or welcome them to your team. After that, well, it could be in any order. Consider two quick case studies:

Felicity

1. Felicity's new manager met with her last week for the first time. She joined the team as the result of a consolidation of departments. In their first one-on-one, the manager asked her about her prior experiences with the company, and they discovered that they both had a strong attachment to data analytics. Felicity expressed

her hope that she would be able to be involved in the analytical components of the team's work.

2. This week the manager met with Felicity again, and she wanted to understand how to come up to speed on the company's proprietary turbo analytics program. The manager sent her off in the direction of team members who could act as mentors and subject matter experts.

3. When the manager bumped into Felicity yesterday, she said that her first interaction with one of the mentors was very challenging. Then she asked for tips on how to better manage the next conversation. The manager coached her on what to do.

The first paragraph beneath the subhead describes an *engage* interaction, followed by *develop* (second paragraph) and then *coach* (third paragraph) in quick succession. Feels like the set of interactions flows naturally, even though the order is different. Here's another example:

Preston

1. Six weeks ago, after a career conversation, Preston's manager sent him to formal training to become a Certified Employee Benefits Specialist. Preston and his manager both agreed that training was needed to fulfill a part of his PDP.

2. The manager saw Preston yesterday and spoke with him about the importance of scheduling time to take practice tests before the final certification exam. The manager had not

noticed Preston studying while in the office and wanted him to understand that he should schedule study time every day.

3. Today, Preston sought out his manager. He was anxious about their previous conversation and needed coaching. Preston was worried that others in the office would think he was goofing off when studying for the CEBS exam. The manager assured Preston that he wanted him to develop, reminded him of how important he was to the team, and encouraged him to not be distracted by others.

In the foregoing scenario, we begin with *develop*, then we move to *coach*, and finally we have a combo *coach/develop/engage* interaction. Again, it's all very natural. The ECD approach can be used in any order you wish and in any combination.

If I have any word of caution, it's that you should be attentive to the observed emotional state of the employee. If the employee is exhibiting a positive, relaxed demeanor, then you have nothing to worry about. But if the employee is exhibiting a negative, agitated demeanor (through either words or body language) and expresses confusion about process and outcome, then you must engineer a different type of conversation.

It's rare that I appeal to common sense, but I will do so in this situation. Whatever reaction you are eliciting from an employee should guide you in what to say or do next—speak, observe, pause, reframe, speak, observe, pause, reframe. This is what I counsel.

Using the ECD Approach with Formal Interaction Models

In the introduction, I spoke about the large number of manager interaction models in existence. I don't bemoan the fact that so many exist, but I do ultimately suggest that there could be a unifying set of principles to help managers better connect with employees. We explored in chapter 1 the basic ideas behind ECD. Then in chapters 2, 3, and 4, we looked at each of those concepts in turn.

Since manager-employee interaction models abound, you really need to pick one and stick with it. Hopefully your organization has already done this for you. In the context of the process suggested by any given model, you can successfully use the ECD *principles*. Here's why you should focus on selecting and adhering to one interaction model:

1. <u>Because both managers and employees need time to practice and improve the skill sets that any one model demands.</u> Trying to improve skill sets using multiple interaction models simultaneously works against the chance of gaining proficiency in a timely way.

2. <u>Because clarity comes from using only one model.</u> It does not take much to create confusion by employing multiple interaction models. Even when the use of multiple models is delineated carefully, a wasteful amount of time and effort is often spent on communicating and recommunicating.

3. <u>Because it is easier and less expensive to enable one interaction model via a standard technology.</u> If your company is large enough, it could choose a full enterprise software application. Some interaction models come with their own technologies and the organization may need to bolt it onto its enterprise system. Or the technology could stand alone.

All things are possible, of course. But why waste your time and effort by using multiple models? You could always adopt one model and then adapt it as needed.

That said, your organization has likely already picked a model for you to use. The model probably outlines a performance management approach, provides a list of competencies or values, and describes the organizational culture. If you don't find anything obvious, then perhaps you can detect the presence of a model by examining the following three common organizational paradigms:

Performance Management

The architecture of your performance management process could itself be the interaction model. Is there a cadence expected for performance conversations? Have any tools, electronic or otherwise, been provided? Have expectations and processes been established for performance or career coaching? Is there a timeline mandating when certain things should happen? If yes, know that these are all indicators of an assumed interaction model.

Behavioral Competencies

The presence of articulated behavioral competencies might also constitute the outline of an interaction model. This is especially true for so-called professional competencies[6] such as communications, teamwork, inclusion, and solutioning. It's not unusual for specified developmental routines to accompany a set of competencies describing how managers should partner with employees to meet behavioral expectations. How those interactions are to be approached is also frequently codified in some way.

---

[6] I advocate that the phrases *professional competencies* and *professional skills* be transformed to *essential competencies*, *essential skills*, or *essential people skills*. Any position requires a set of essential skills that can be codified, explained, and expanded upon. Using the word *professional* suggests that some competencies or skills are *not* professional. This makes little sense to me and causes unnecessary friction.

Culture and Values

The artifacts of your organization's culture may also provide clues to the manager-employee relationship, and what good interactions look and sound like. For example, values can sometimes look suspiciously like competencies. If one of your organization's values is collaboration, then within the text describing it, you are likely to find an articulation of expected behaviors. The description could be general for all employees or specific to the manager-employee relationship. The same goes for culture. If there are descriptions of what the organizational culture is or should be, you will find the elements of an interaction model present too, I'm betting.

A few years ago, I was asked to consult with a midsized services company. Such a great organization! They were interested in my thoughts on how to integrate competencies, values, and performance management into a consistent behavior and process model that all employees could understand and benefit from. You see, they did not have an explicit manager-employee interaction model, but they did have many helpful descriptions of expectations and of what good, better, and best looked like. There was plenty to work with! In the end, I proposed a "decoder ring" approach where individuals could self-navigate across the three main content streams. Managers needed training on how to do that, but it was the most straightforward answer to their question, I felt.

Manager Interaction Models that Deserve a Close Look

Below are some of my favorite interaction models. I only name them here, with a few brief comments. I'm not endorsing any one of them *per se* since each organization needs to select a model that will drive its business strategy and desired outcomes. However, you should assume that I think all these models have merit and sit comfortably in an ECD approach. I picked the following four models by assessing them against a simple set of criteria:

1. The model is easy to explain, which reduces communications and change management effort.
2. The model includes process steps and flow, which eases implementation and plays to most personality styles.
3. The model is based on valuable research into management or psychology, which assists with credibility and increases the likelihood of buy-in.
4. The model is well-documented and available in multiple media formats, which allows for speed when the need is great.

Steve King

I've mentioned King's models a few times already. His books *Six Conversations* (2015) and *Brag, Worry, Wonder, Bet* (2013) both provide simple interaction models for managers and employees to take advantage of. I like the simplicity and focus afforded by King's two models. Every student I've ever had in a classroom in which these models were featured snapped them up quickly and applied them efficiently.

Patrick Lencioni

The five behaviors identified by Lencioni in his team effectiveness model are also critical for one-on-one interactions. In Lencioni's now-famous leadership fable described in his book *The Five Dysfunctions of a Team* (2002), he proposes five behaviors: trust, conflict (management), commitment, accountability, and results. He also provides a very useful diagnostic tool that can be used productively with his model called the Five Behaviors Team Development Profile. The Lencioni organization and the DiSC profile organization have developed a joint assessment that I find very intriguing. You should check it out.

Daniel Pink

This model consists of three important elements that Pink attaches to the broad topic of employee motivation. The elements are autonomy, mastery, and purpose. I really like Pink's framework and have used it in a classroom setting many times. Pink's book *Drive: The Surprising Truth about What Motivates Us* (2011) will provide everything you need to know about this model.

David Rock

The model developed by Rock consists of six steps whose hoped-for outcome is improved employee performance. Rock has written extensively about how the brain operates and the ways in which we can reach our greatest potential. The six steps describe what managers should concentrate on when interacting with employees: (1) think about thinking, (2) listen for potential, (3) speak with intent, (4) dance toward insight, (5) create new thinking, and (6) follow up. You can read all about Rock's model in his book *Quiet Leadership: Six Steps to Transforming Performance at Work* (2007).

Last Thing

I've seen managers over the years become so severely twisted up in the process of interacting with their employees that they forget the most important aspect: spending time with their employees! Use a model if one is available from your organization or pick a model that suits you and the employees well. But there is no replacement for simply spending time with employees. ECD can help you to know the topics to cover, but that's not what employees will remember. In looking back upon a conversation with you, they will recall most readily how you made them feel.

AFTERWORD

I'm going to immediately reveal my bias: It's all about *engage*. Without engage, nothing much happens, at least not on a genuine level or in a sustainable way.

We all have a deep need to be heard and understood. When we aren't, it's like being without oxygen—it's all we can think about, and it guides our every action.

When we don't feel heard and understood, we aren't open to coaching, development, influence, or change of any type. Why? Because we don't feel safe. And people who don't feel safe defend, deflect, and disengage.

But building relationships—and the safety that is created—isn't easy in the workplace. It never was, and it certainly isn't now that we're working more globally and virtually. At work, we have the relational deck stacked against us. Think about your relationships outside of work for a moment. The faces and names that come to mind likely have three common elements:

- Proximity
  Now you have, or at some point you had, physical proximity with the person.

- Chemistry
  You connect or have a commonality that brought you together.

- Time
  The relationship was built over time.

At work, we are often missing all three of the foregoing elements. We are down the hall, on another campus, or across the ocean from each other (there goes proximity); we may have nothing in common (chemistry is lacking); and we often don't have the time to let the relationship naturally take hold.

In other words, our work relationships don't grow organically. They only grow through our deliberate effort.

So, as Artell states, it requires a **steady effort to connect deeply**. And just when I think I couldn't agree more, he pulls out my favorite word: *curiosity*.

Expressing genuine curiosity is one of the greatest gifts you can give someone. It is a totally underrated leadership quality. And it is imperative to engaging with others. In that split second when we are inclined to judge or discount or assume, we can choose to pause and get curious. When we get curious, we are better leaders, partners, and parents—just better humans.

My advice to you is to get curious and focus on **engage**. When you start there, all chosen models work.

Susan Finerty

Susan Finerty is the author of the following books:

- *Cross-Functional Influence: Getting Things Done across the Organization* (2019)
- *Cross-Functional Influence Playbook* (2019)
- *Master the Matrix: Getting Things Done in Complex Organizations* (3rd ed., 2022)

SOURCES

Allen, James B. *As a Man Thinketh*. New York: Simon & Schuster, 1903.

Bar-On, Reuven, and James D. A. Parker, eds. *The Handbook of Emotional Intelligence: The Theory and Practice of Development, Evaluation, Education, and Application—at Home, at School, and in the Workplace*. San Francisco: Jossey-Bass, 2000.

Bedford, Christopher. "The Role of Learning Agility in Workplace Performance and Career Advancement." PhD diss., University of Minnesota, 2011.

Carnegie, Dale. *How to Win Friends and Influence People*. New York: Simon & Schuster, 1998.

Covey, Steven R. *The 7 Habits of Highly Effective People*. 30th ed. New York: Simon & Schuster, 2020.

———. *Spiritual Roots of Human Relations*. Salt Lake City: Deseret Book Company, 1970.

Drucker, Peter. *Management: Tasks, Responsibilities, and Practices*. New York: Harper & Row, 1974.

Finerty, Susan. *Cross-Functional Influence: Getting Things Done across the Organization.* Minneapolis: Two Harbors Press, 2019.

———. *Cross-Functional Influence Playbook.* Minneapolis: Two Harbors Press, 2019.

———. *Master the Matrix: Getting Things Done in Complex Organizations.* 3rd ed. Minneapolis: Two Harbors Press, 2022.

Grieser, Randy, Eric Stutzman, Wendy Loewen, and Troy Labun. *The Culture Question: How to Create a Workplace Where People Like to Work.* Winnipeg, Manitoba, Canada: Achieve, 2019.

Goleman, Daniel. *Emotional Intelligence: Why It Can Matter More than IQ.* 25th ed. London: Bloomsbury, 2020.

Gubman, Edward. *The Talent Solution: Aligning Strategy and People to Achieve Extraordinary Results.* New York: McGraw Hill, 1993.

King, Steve. *Alignment, Process, Relationships: A Simple Guide to Team Management.* Bloomington, IN: iUniverse, 2019.

———. *Brag, Worry, Wonder, Bet: A Manager's Guide to Giving Feedback.* Bloomington, IN: iUniverse, 2013.

———. *The Manager's Dilemma: A Manager's Guide to Change Management.* Bloomington, IN: iUniverse, 2022.

———. *Six Conversations: A Simple Guide for Managerial Success.* Bloomington, IN: iUniverse, 2015.

Meyer, Nicholas, dir. *Star Trek II: The Wrath of Khan.* Hollywood, CA: Paramount Home Entertainment, 2009. DVD.

Nimoy, Leonard, dir. *Star Trek III: The Search for Spock*. Hollywood, CA: Paramount Pictures, 2002. DVD.

Peale, Norman Vincent. *The Power of Positive Thinking*. New York: Simon & Schuster, 2015.

Pink, Daniel. *Drive: The Surprising Truth about What Motivates Us*. New York: Riverhead Hardcover, 2009.

Rock, David P. *Quiet Leadership: Six Steps to Transforming Performance at Work*. New York: Harper Business, 2007.

Seppälä, Emma. *The Happiness Track: How to Apply the Science of Happiness to Accelerate Your Success*. Reprint, San Francisco: Harper One, 2017

Singh, Deanna. *Actions Speak Louder: A Step-by-Step Guide to Becoming an Inclusive Workplace*. New York: Penguin Random House, 2022.

Winters, Mary-Frances. *Black Fatigue*. Oakland, CA: Berrett-Koehler, 2020.

———. *Inclusive Conversations*. Oakland, CA: Berrett-Koehler, 2020.

———. *We Can't Talk about That at Work*. Oakland, CA: Berrett-Koehler, 2017.

Zenger, Jack, and Joe Folkman. *The New Extraordinary Leader: Turning Good Managers into Great Leaders*. 3rd ed. New York: McGraw-Hill, 2019.

INDEX

D

develop. *See also* ECD approach
    as element of ECD
        approach, 5–6
    examples of questions used
        in, 9
    how to develop your
        employees, 43–53
DiSC profile organization, 61
discouragement, among
    managers, 1–2
dismay, among managers, 2
*Drive: The Surprising Truth about
    What Motivates Us* (Pink),
    2, 62
Drucker, Peter, xvi, xvii

E

ECD approach
    benefits of using, 6
    elements of, 4–6
    example of, 6–7
    use of with formal interaction
        models, 57–60
efficiency, defined, xvi–xvii
emotional intelligence
    core mandates of, 35
    making it your superpower,
        34–36
*Emotional Intelligence: Why It
    Can Matter More than IQ*
    (Goleman), 34
employees
    discovering the right and most
        important skills for,
        47–48
    getting to know motives of,
        20–24
    how to develop yours, 43–53

learning to enjoy who they are
    right now, 31–33
questions to help you get to
    know and enjoy your
    coachee, 33–34
valuing the person and the
    relationship more than
    the desired skills, 36–37
working with angry ones, 17–18
working with introverted
    ones, 17
working with suspicious ones,
    17–18
engage/engagement. *See also* ECD
    approach
    author's bias toward, 63
    defined, 3
    as element of ECD approach, 4
    example of effort to that
        started well and ended
        badly, 18–19
    example of regular engage
        process, 16
    examples of questions used
        in, 8
    simple process for, 13–16

F

fatigue, among managers, 2
"First, Let's Fire All the Managers"
    (Harnel), xviii
Five Behaviors Team Development
    Profile, 61
The Five Dysfunctions of a Team
    (Lencioni), 61
Folkman, Joe, 5
Freud, Sigmund, 46

G

Goleman, Daniel, 34
Grieser, Randy, 36

Printed in the United States
by Baker & Taylor Publisher Services